Berger Science Readers

CHOMP!

A Book About
Sharks

For the boys and girls
of the E.M. Baker School
— M.B. and G.B.

Special thanks to Laurie Roulston
of the Denver Museum of Natural History
for her expertise

Photography credits:

Cover: James D. Watt/Seapics.com; Back: Mark Strickland/Seapics.com; Pages: 3: James D. Watt/Seapics.com; 4: Ben Cropp/Seapics.com; 5: Norbert Wu; 6: Chris Crumley Productions, Inc.; 7: Bill Curtsinger Photography; 8-9: Mark Conlin/Seapics.com; 10: Ron and Valerie Taylor/Seapics.com; 11: Walt Stearns/Seapics.com; 12: Norbert Wu/Peter Arnold, Inc.; 13: Bill Curtsinger Photography; 14:Doug Perrine & Jose Castro/Seapics.com; 15: Bill Curtsinger Photography; 17: Michael S. Nolan/Seapics.com; 18: Jozon/Seapics.com; 19: Doug Perrine/Seapics.com; 20: Mark Strickland/Seapics.com; 21: Jeff Rotman; 22: Jeff Rotman; 23: Jeff Rotman; 24: McConnaughey/Photo Researchers; 25: Mark Strickland/Seapics.com; 26: Doug Perrine/Seapics.com; 27: Mark Conlin/Seapics.com; 28: Massimo & Lucia Simon/Jeff Rotman; 29: Jeff Rotman; 30: Jeff Rotman/ Seapics.com; 31: David B. Fleetham/ Seapics.com; 32: Doug Perrine/Seapics.com; 33: Bill Curtsinger Photography; 34: J. Dan Wright/EarthWater Stock Photography; 35(top): Norbert Wu; 35(bottom): Norbert Wu; 36: Douglas David Seifert; 37: Bob Cranston/Seapics. com; 38: N. Marsh/ Seapics.com; 39: Mark Conlin/Seapics.com. Photo Research: Sarah Longacre

ISBN: 0-439-80184-2

Text copyright © 2006, 1999 by Melvin and Gilda Berger
All rights reserved. Published by Scholastic Inc.
SCHOLASTIC and associated logos
are trademarks and/or registered trademarks of Scholastic Inc.

12 11 10 9 8 7 6 5 4   6 7 8 9 10 11/0
Printed in the U.S.A.
First revised edition, February 2006

Berger Science Readers

CHOMP!

A Book About Sharks

by Melvin & Gilda Berger

SCHOLASTIC INC.

New York Toronto London Auckland Sydney
Mexico City New Delhi Hong Kong Buenos Aires

Chapter One

Great Hunters

Sharks are the most feared fish in the sea. They eat any animal they can find. Some big sharks even eat small sharks!

All sharks are great hunters. They also have huge appetites. Yet most sharks only eat one big meal every two or three days.

A hungry shark swims slowly back and forth. Its senses are wide awake.

Suddenly, the shark smells something. It is blood in the water. The blood is about a mile away. That's as long as 20 blocks. The shark speeds toward the smell.

The shark also picks up some faraway sounds. The shark's ears are two small holes on the sides of its head. It hears something moving in the water. The shark swims even faster.

The water is dark. But the shark
sees well in little light. It spots an
injured seal. The seal has been badly
cut. There is blood in the water.

The shark circles around. It comes
in closer and closer. Suddenly, the

shark lunges. *CHOMP!* It sinks its teeth into the seal.

The shark rips off a large chunk of flesh. *GULP!* The shark swallows it whole.

All at once, other sharks appear. They churn and stir up the water. Each wants the same seal.

The sharks snap and rip at the seal. They bite one another. Sometimes they even bite themselves! It's called a "feeding frenzy."

Soon there is little left of the seal. The feeding frenzy is over. The sharks glide away.

Most sharks hunt fish, seals, and porpoises. Some eat dead or dying animals and shellfish. A few kinds of sharks feed on very tiny sea plants and animals.

Chapter Two

Powerful Swimmers

Sharks seem made for swimming. Most have sleek, rounded bodies. They slip easily through the water.

Sharks use their fins to swim. They swing their big tail fin from side to side. The tail pushes against the water. It moves the shark forward.

The shark has two side fins. They look like small airplane wings. These fins help the shark turn and make sudden stops. They also raise the shark up in the water. The big fin on its back keeps the shark from rolling over.

Sharks do not have smooth scales like most fish. Instead they have many sharp, pointed scales. The points face back toward the tail. They help water flow over the shark's body—without slowing it down.

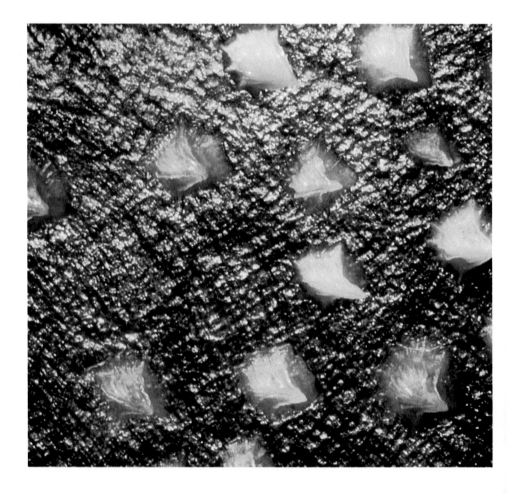

Sharks usually swim about three miles per hour. But they can put on bursts of speed. Some reach 40 miles per hour when hunting!

Did you know that most sharks swim all the time? They swim day and night. They even swim while they're asleep!

Swimming and breathing go together. If sharks stop swimming, they stop breathing and they die.

Sharks breathe oxygen (OCK-si-jun). We breathe oxygen, too. Our oxygen comes from the air. Sharks get their oxygen from the water.

Most sharks swim with open mouths. The water flows in. It passes over gill slits on the sharks' sides. The gills take oxygen from the water. Then the water flows out.

Swimming also keeps sharks afloat. If they stop swimming, they sink to the bottom.

A shark twists and turns as it swims. That's because it doesn't have a bone in its body! A shark's skeleton is made of cartilage (CAR-tuh-lij). And cartilage bends easily.

Your nose and ears have cartilage. Try it out. Do you see how easily you can bend them?

Sharks often swim with two types of trusty friends. One is the **pilot fish**. Pilot fish seem to lead the sharks. But all they do is catch food that the sharks drop.

The other shark friend is the
remora. Remoras hitch rides on sharks.
They also eat any small sea animals
that dig into sharks' skin. No wonder
sharks don't seem to mind remoras
tagging along.

Chapter Three

Hundreds of Teeth

Sharks have lots of teeth.
Some have hundreds. A few have
thousands. Imagine brushing that
many teeth twice a day!

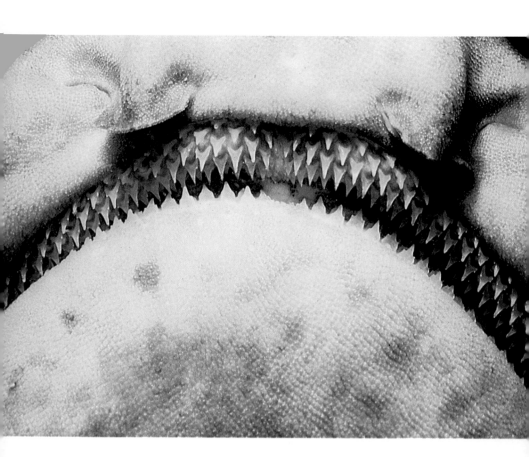

Sharks' teeth are fit for what sharks eat.

- Curved teeth are for biting.
- Pointed teeth are for catching small fish.
- Flat teeth are for crushing shellfish.

When a shark is ready to eat, it lifts its snout. This pushes the shark's mouth out in front. It also bares its teeth.

Shark teeth are not all in one row like yours. Most sharks have several rows of teeth. Others have up to 300 rows. The rows are behind each other in the shark's jaw.

Usually the shark uses only the front rows for biting. Their teeth do not have roots like your teeth. After about two weeks, the front row falls out or breaks off. Then a new row from behind takes its place.

The rows of teeth move forward like steps on an escalator. They go from the back of the jaw to the front.

Sharks can lose thousands of teeth in a lifetime. Divers find many on the ocean floor. Sailors used to shave with them!

Chapter Four

Fantastic Babies

Shark babies are called pups.
Shark mothers usually give birth to a
few pups at a time.

All pups grow from eggs. In most sharks, the eggs grow inside the mother. They can grow there for nearly a year.

When ready, the pups come out of the mother's body. But they're not like human babies. Pups take care of themselves from the start. Off they go to hunt for food.

Some mother sharks lay eggs outside their bodies. The eggs are in cases. The cases fall to the bottom of the sea.

The pup grows inside the egg case. It takes as long as ten months to hatch. When it hatches, the pup swims out—and away!

Sometimes egg cases wash ashore. People find them on the beach. They call the cases "mermaids' purses."

Chapter Five

Curious Creatures

Sharks live all over the world. They live in deep water and shallow water. They live in cold water and warm water. Some even live in rivers and lakes.

Nearly everyone is afraid of sharks. Yet most sharks rarely harm us. In the whole world, only about 50 people are attacked by sharks in a year.

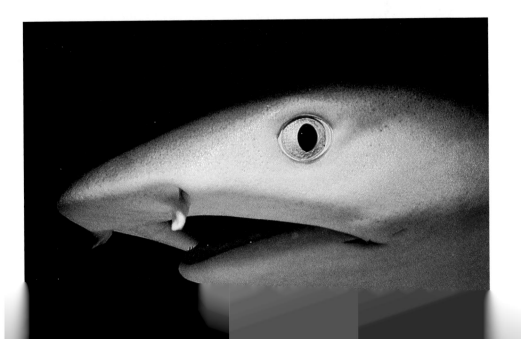

The most dangerous shark is the **great white.** It swims mainly in deep, cold seas. Its underside is white. But its back is dark.

The shark's colors make the great white hard to see. From below, the shark looks light like the sky. From above, the shark looks dark like the water.

Large fish, seals, sea lions, and even other sharks are food for the great white shark.

The **bull shark** is mostly found in shallow water. Sometimes it swims into rivers or lakes. A short snout and stout body make it look like a bull. That's how it got its name.

The **blue shark** is easy to spot. It swims near the surface of the ocean. Its big back fin pokes up out of the water. Blues mostly swim together in large groups.

Some people call the **tiger shark** a "swimming garbage can." It will eat just about anything. A fisherman once caught a tiger shark. In its belly, he found nine shoes, a belt, and a pair of pants!

One of the smallest sharks is the **dwarf shark**. It is only about six inches long. You could hold one in your hand.

The biggest shark is the **whale shark**. It can be as long and heavy as a tractor trailer! Sometimes the whale shark stands upright in the water. It bobs up and down, swallowing whole schools of small fish.

The **hammerhead shark** looks odd, to say the least. It has a thick bar across the front of its head. Its eyes are at the ends of the bar.

The hammerhead's bar also has the shark's nostrils for smelling. The nostrils help the hammerhead find the fish, crabs, and stingrays that it eats.

It's easy to mistake the **carpet shark** for a rug. It lies flat and still on the ocean floor. Fringe around its snout makes it look even more ruglike. But let a fish swim by. The carpet shark whips around and grabs it!

The **angel shark** is no angel.
It digs its body into the sand or hides
in reefs or caves under the water.
But nearby shellfish had better be
careful. The angel shark is always
ready to pounce.

Now you know that sharks:
- are mighty hunters,
- are powerful swimmers,
- have lots of teeth,
- give birth to pups,
- live almost everywhere,
- and come in all sizes and shapes.

Sharks are really amazing!

Index